Also by Barry Sheinkopf

POETRY

Not That I Minded
Live From The Limelight
Collected Poems
What There Was

FICTION

The Longest Odds
The Ivory Kitten
These Barely Silent Dead

NONFICTION

The Magic Pencil: How A Jewish Art Restorer Survived The Holocaust
Make It Good: The Stories in My Early Life

PHOTOGRAPHS

Life Forms: Photographing Metaphor

A Healing Eye

*Images and Words
in a Time of Plague*

Barry Sheinkopf

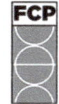

Full Court Press
Englewood Cliffs, New Jersey

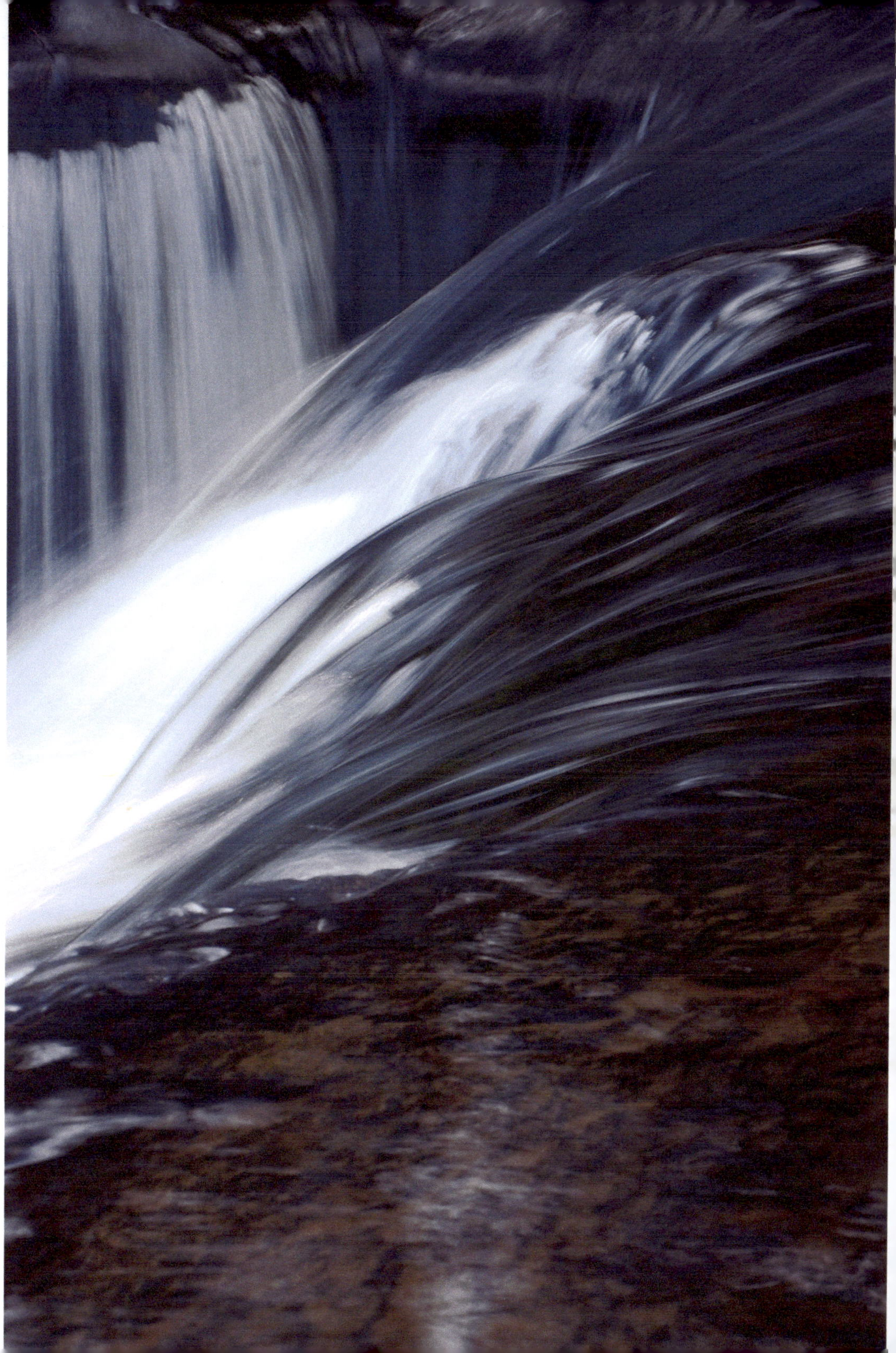

First Edition

Copyright © 2020 by Barry Sheinkopf

All rights reserved. No part of this book may be
reproduced or transmitted in any form or by any means
electronic or mechanical, including by
photocopying, by recording, or by any information storage
and retrieval system, without the express
permission of the author,
except where permitted by law.

Published in the United States of America
by Full Court Press, 601 Palisade Avenue,
Englewood Cliffs, NJ 07632
fullcourtpress.com

ISBN 978-1-946989-65-9

Book design, and all art, by the author

AUTHOR'S NOTE

We are living through a very grim time—with death lurking invisibly all around us, livelihoods shaken or destroyed, emotions running wild in all directions, governments struggling with varying degrees of integrity and success to contain the mayhem, and our very nature as social creatures held in cautious check.

We're calling the microscopic organism that has attacked us Coronavirus and the disease it causes Covid-19, but it's a plague plain and simple: novel, horrifying, highly contagious, perhaps recurring. Our future has become uncertain, a mystery.

That's why I have subtitled this collection *Images and Words in a Time of Plague*. I've been using cameras for a long time, living with the astonishment of the world around me and trying to capture, not just the *facts* of what I see, but that very astonishment.

I offer some of those images here—like candles set adrift in a river on paper plates—wedded to insights they have called to mind that poets and writers have left us over many centuries. I offer the book in the hope that it sustains you as these images have sustained me with the faith that the joy of living will endure for us all—that, as Kafka once put it, "They threw us out of Paradise, but Paradise was not destroyed."

For the living, and in memory of the dead

"The question is not what you look at, but what you see."
—Henry David Thoreau

All the birds have flown up and gone;
A cloud floats leisurely by.

The mountain and I never tire
of looking at each other—
Until there is only the mountain.

—Li Po

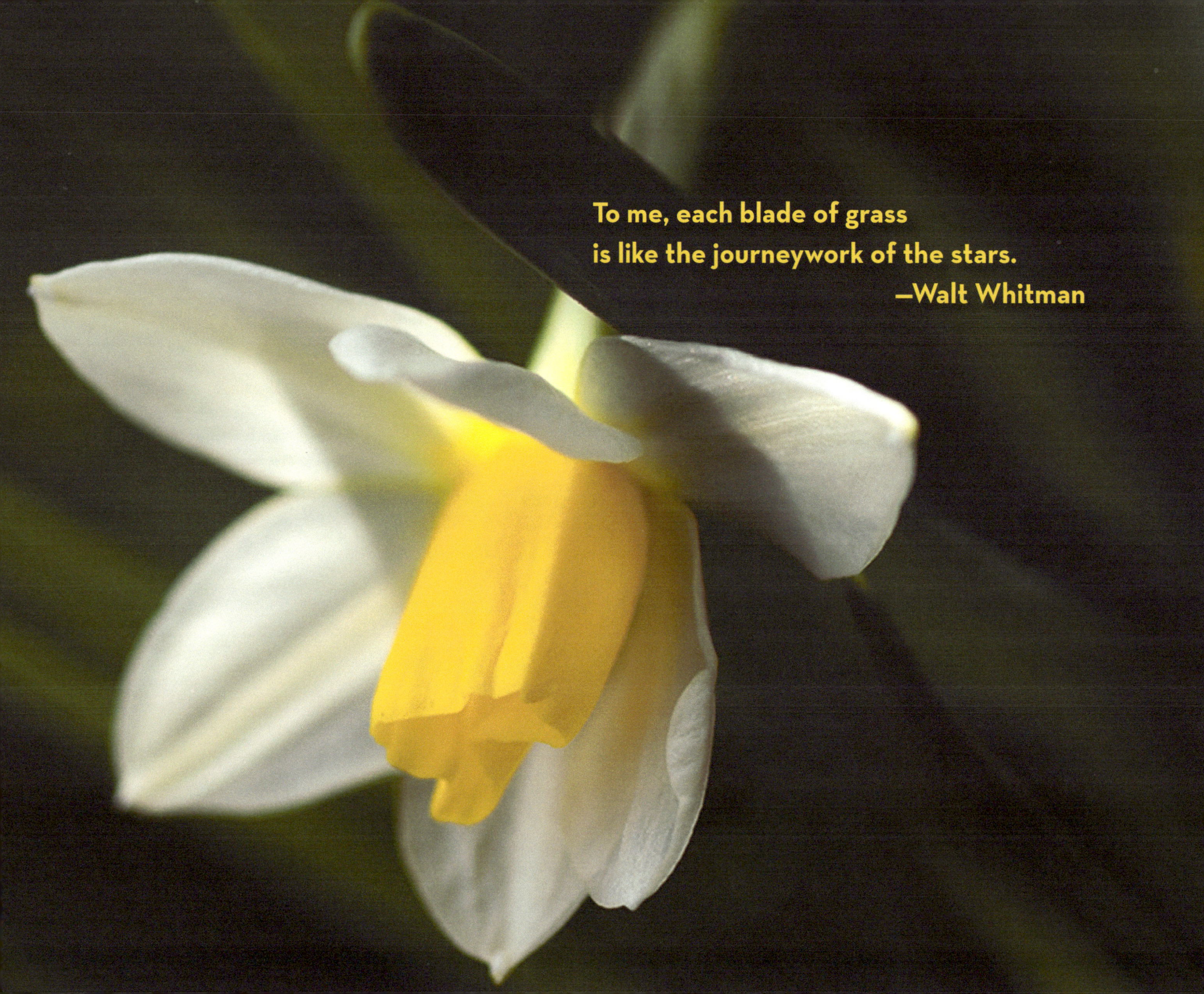

To me, each blade of grass
is like the journeywork of the stars.
—Walt Whitman

Money and office and success are the consolations of impotence. Fortune turns kind to such solid people and lets them suck their bone in peace. She flicks her whip upon flesh that is more alive, upon that stream of hungry boys and girls who are the Future, and who possess the treasure of creative power.

—Willa Cather

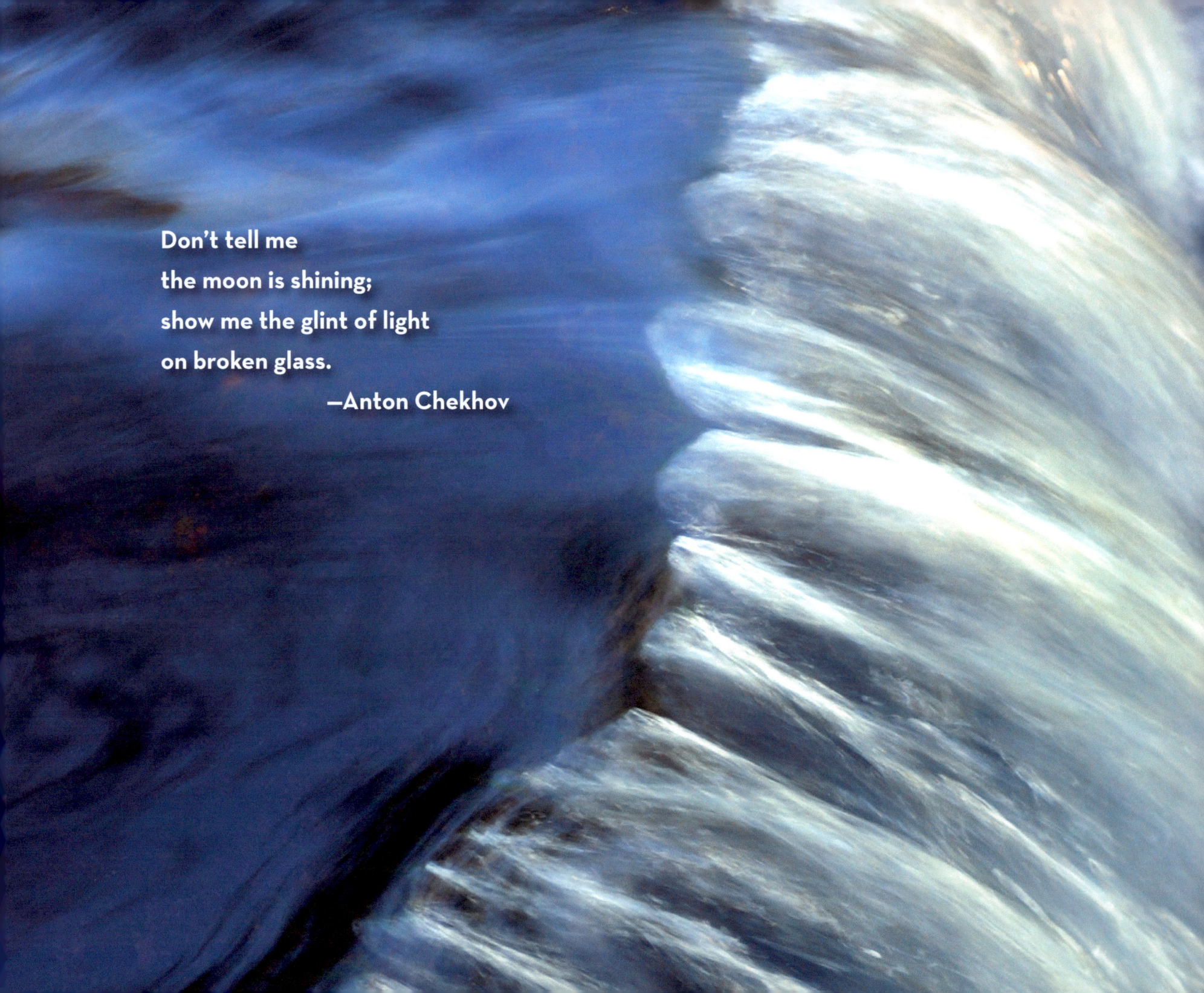

> The dead return to places they treasured in life to collect footsteps. These became a shrine to all the happier times on Earth.
>
> —Laotian legend

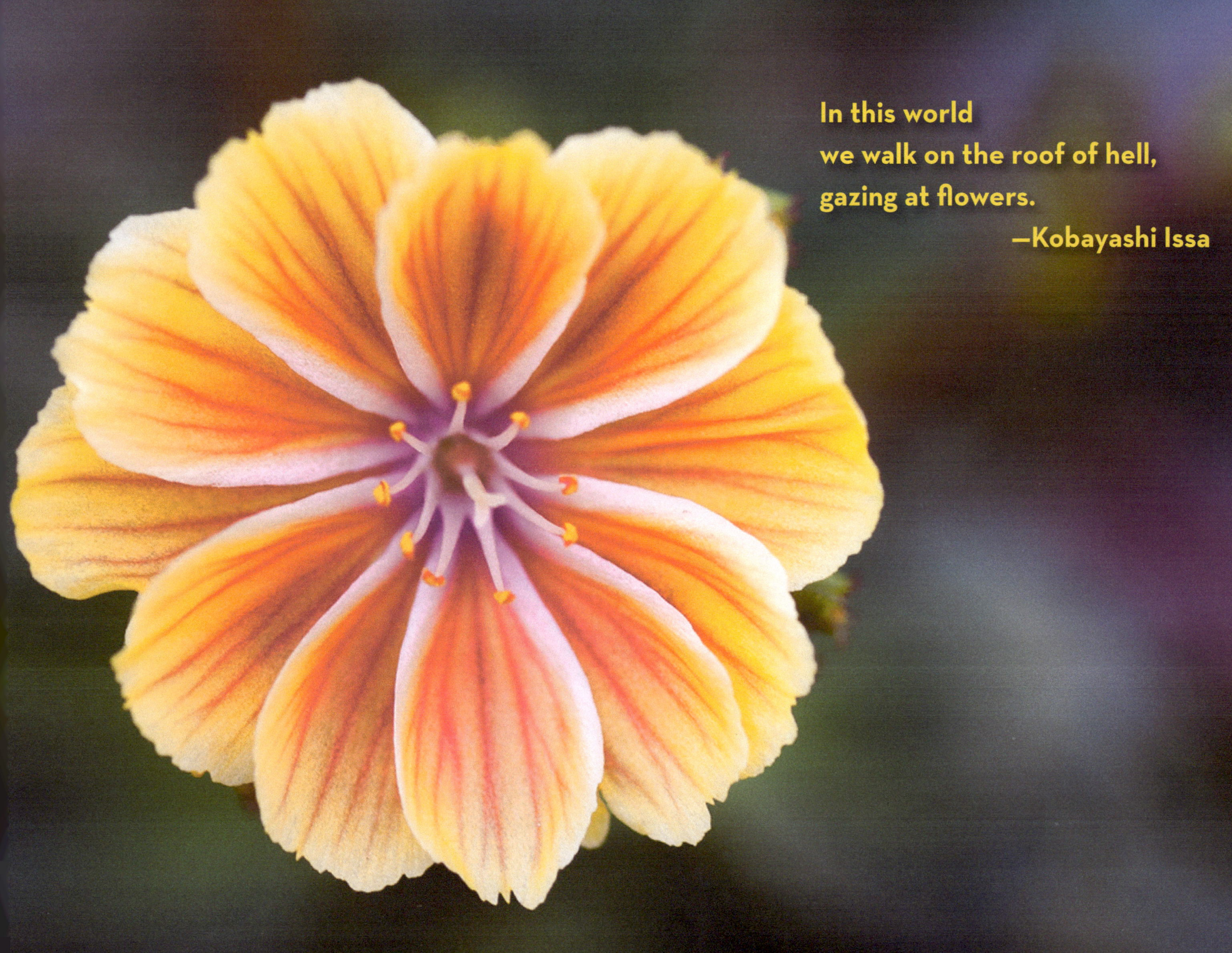

In this world
we walk on the roof of hell,
gazing at flowers.
—Kobayashi Issa

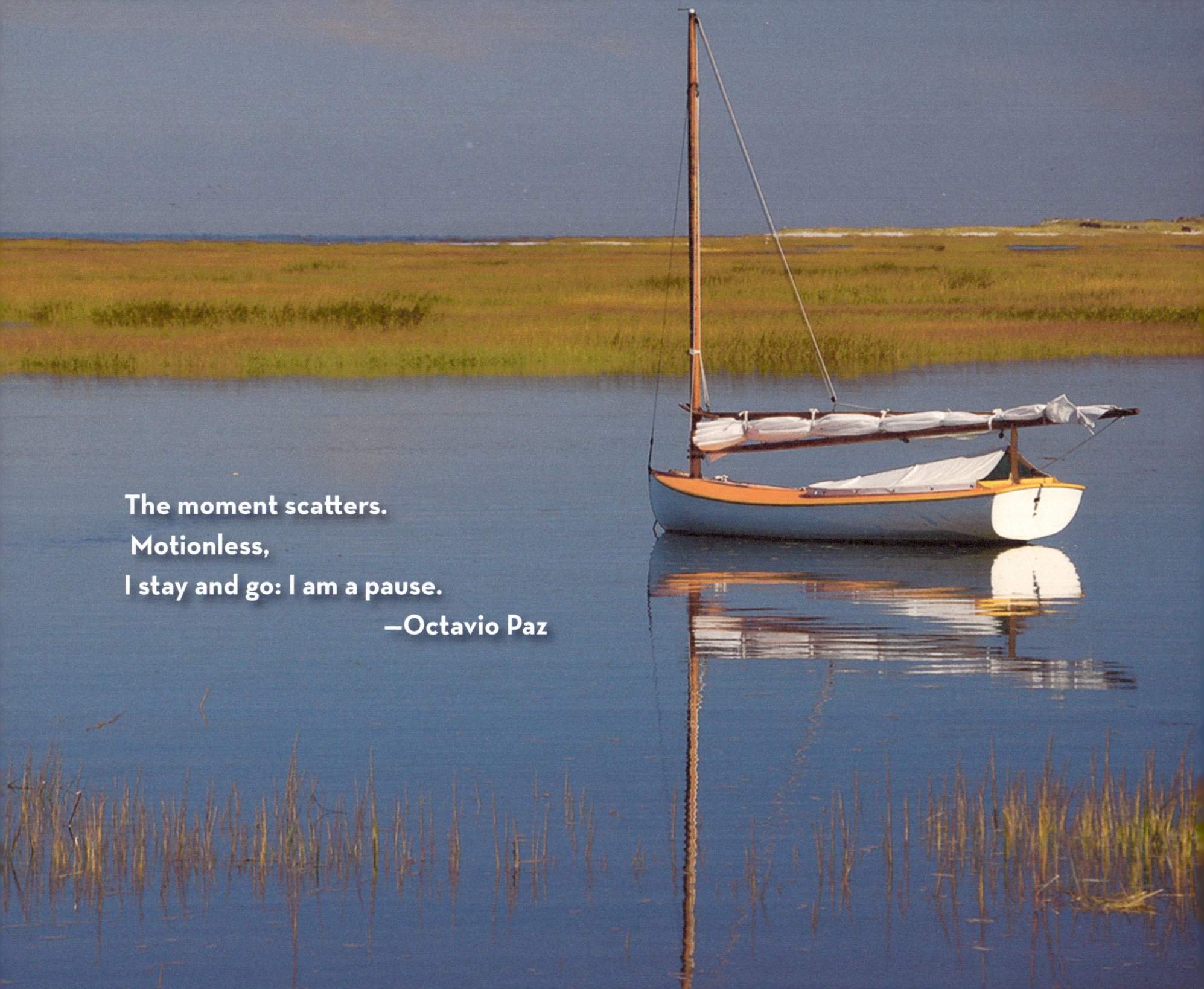

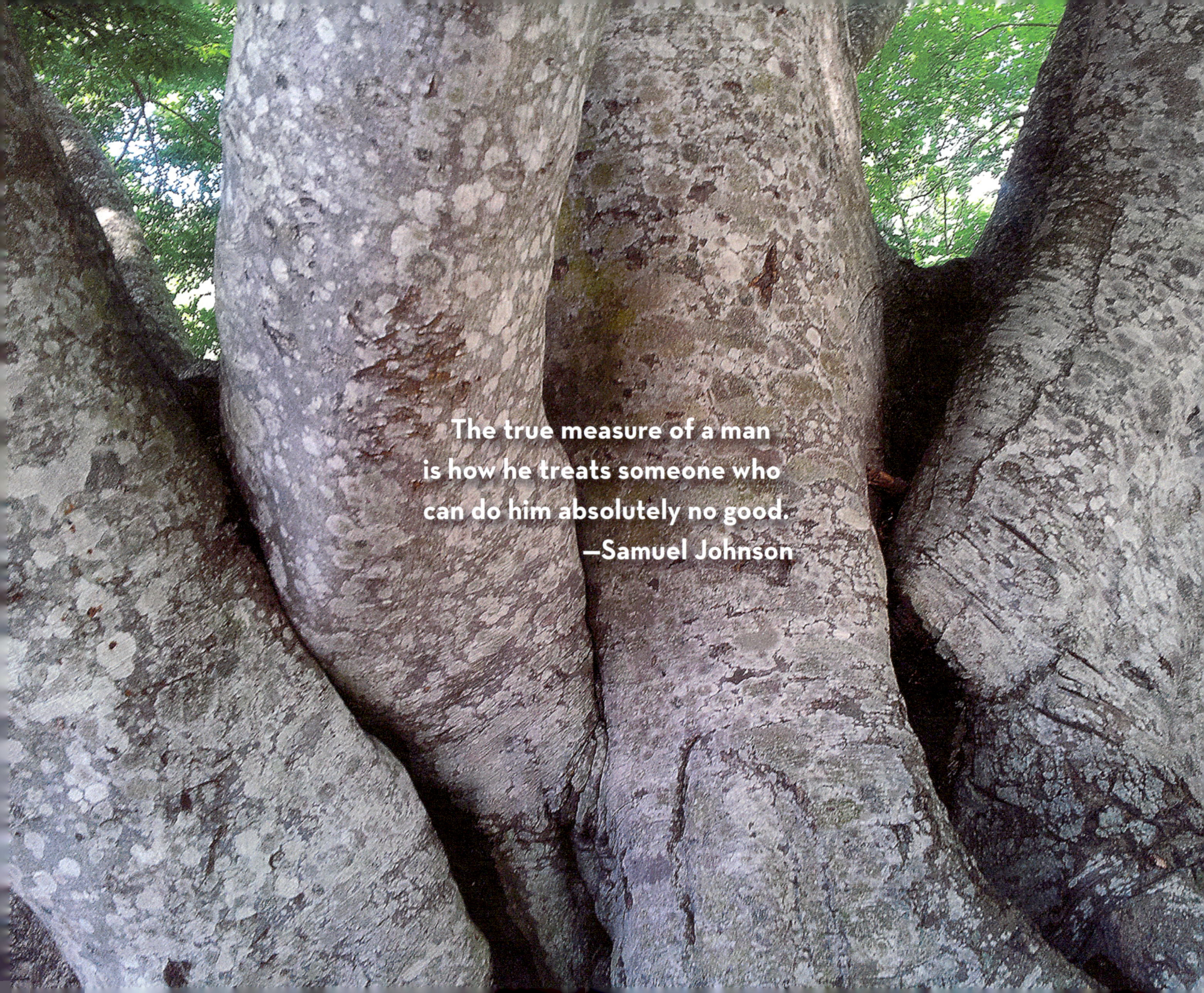

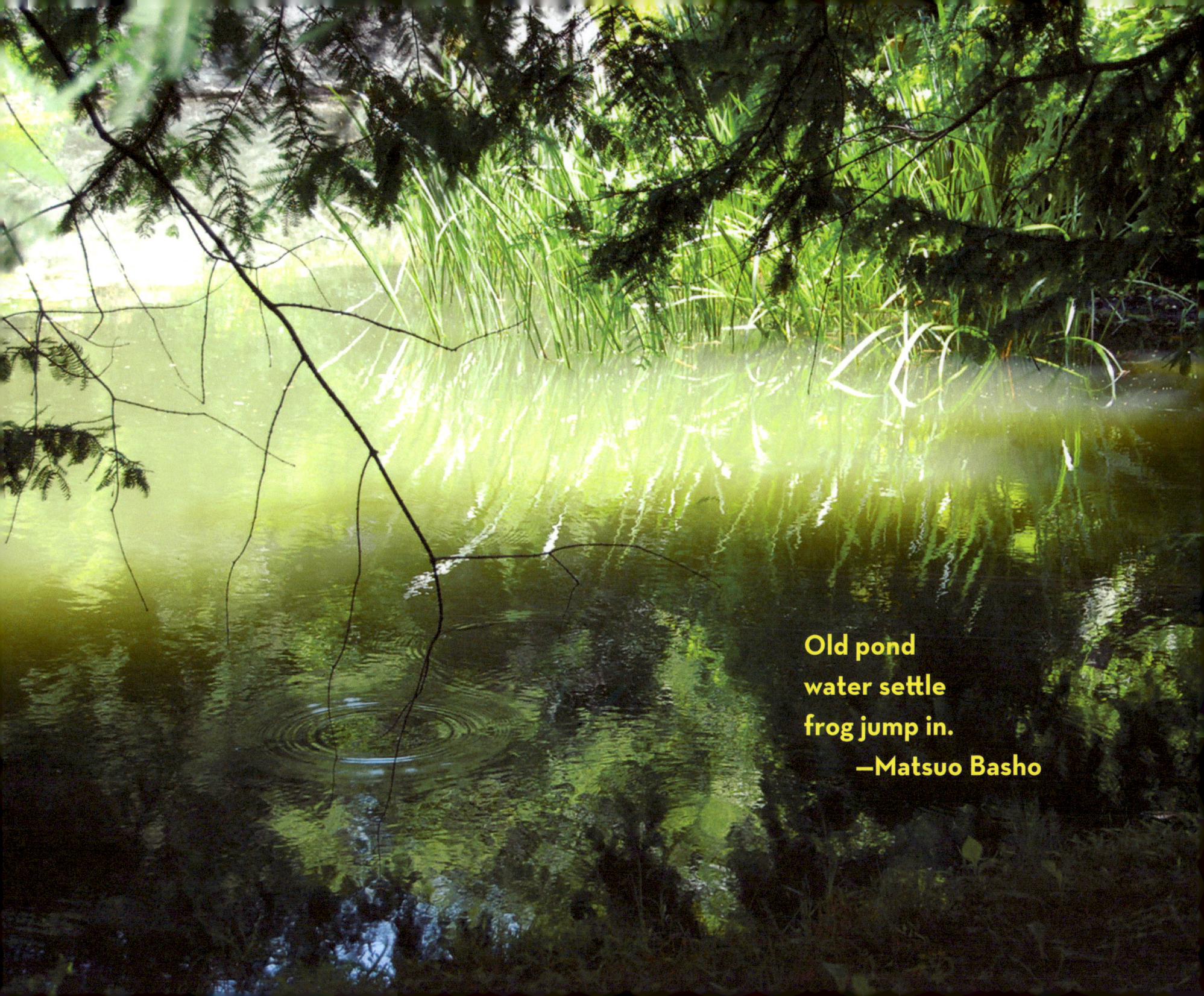

Old pond
water settle
frog jump in.
—Matsuo Basho

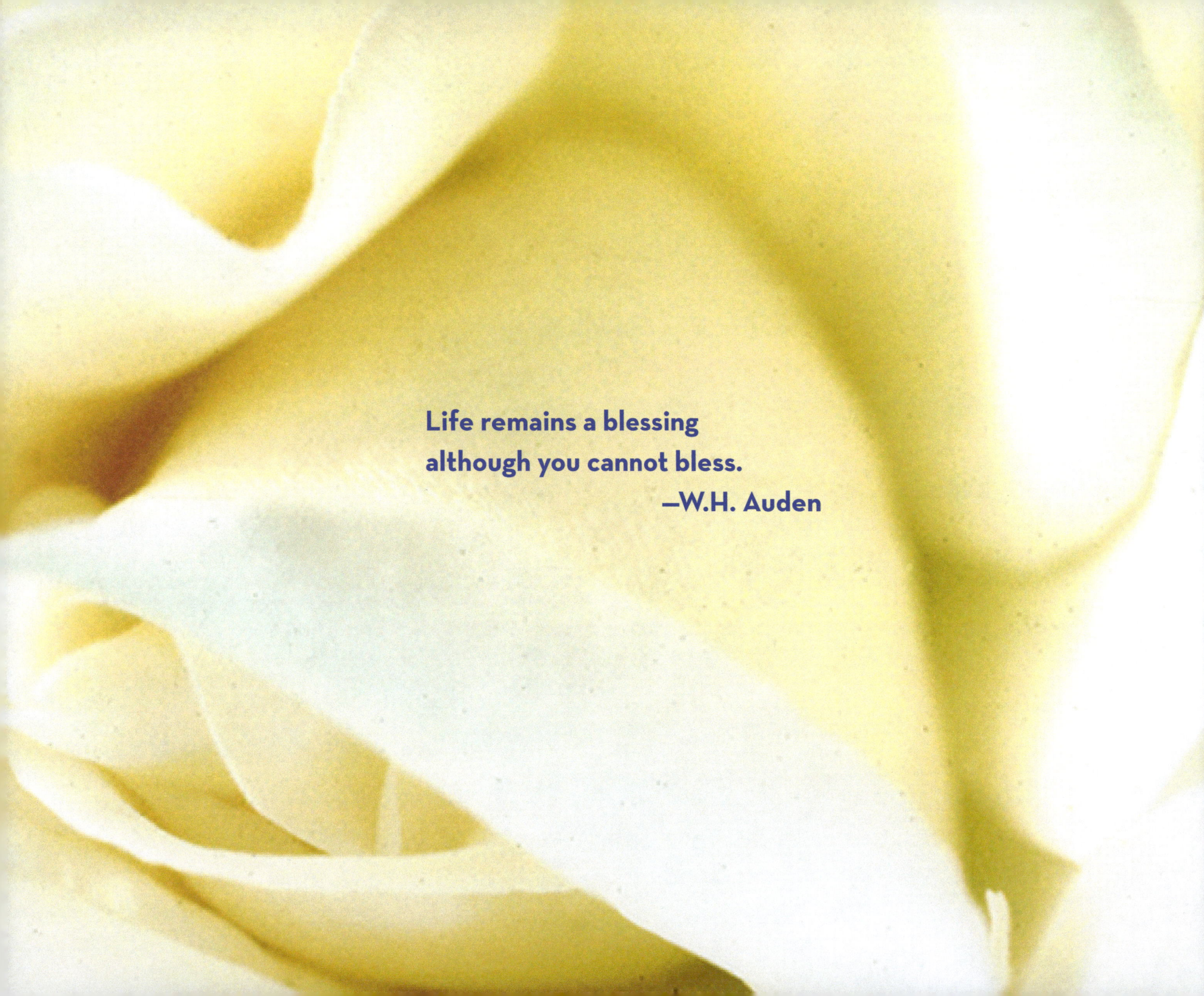

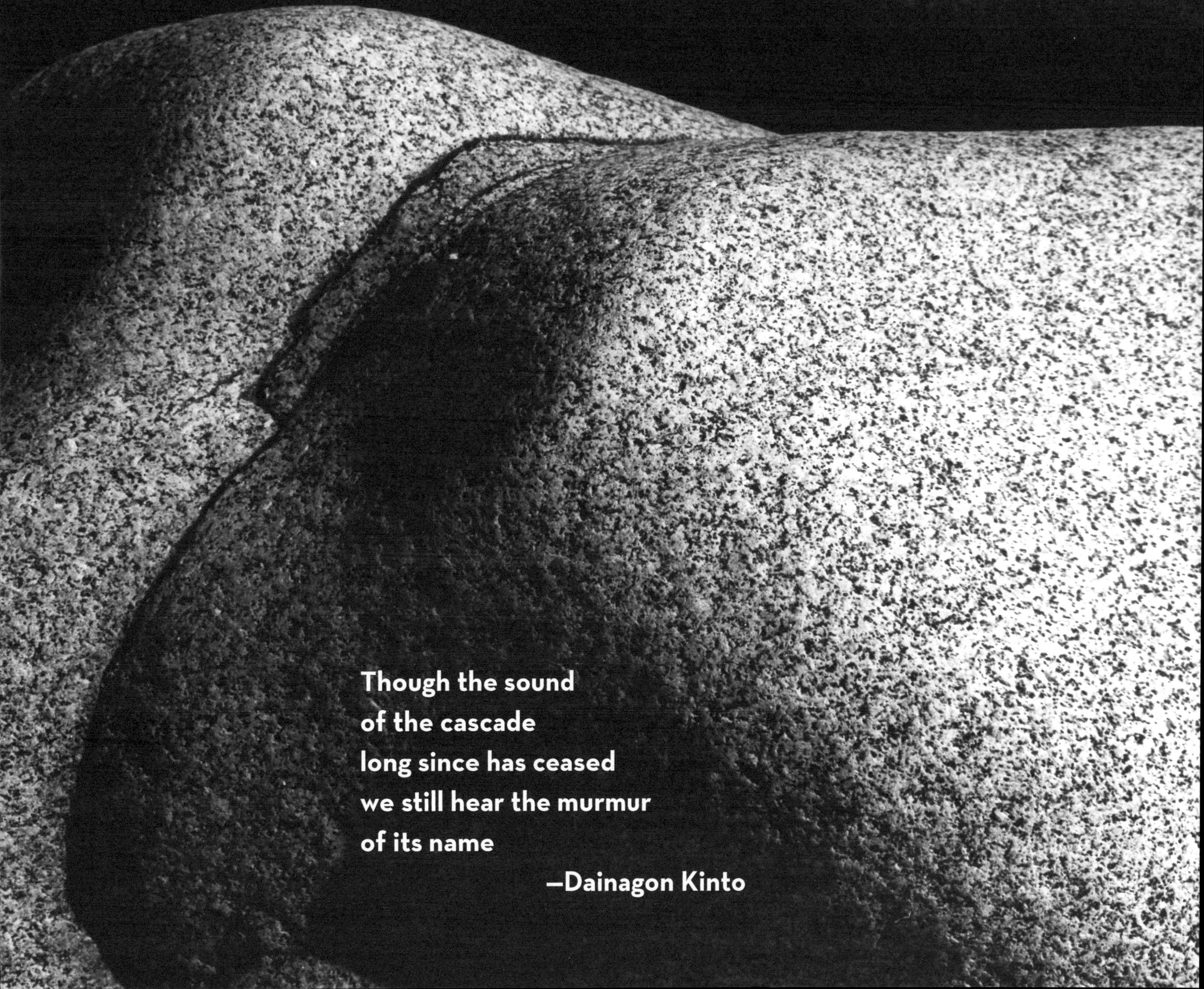

Though the sound
of the cascade
long since has ceased
we still hear the murmur
of its name

—Dainagon Kinto

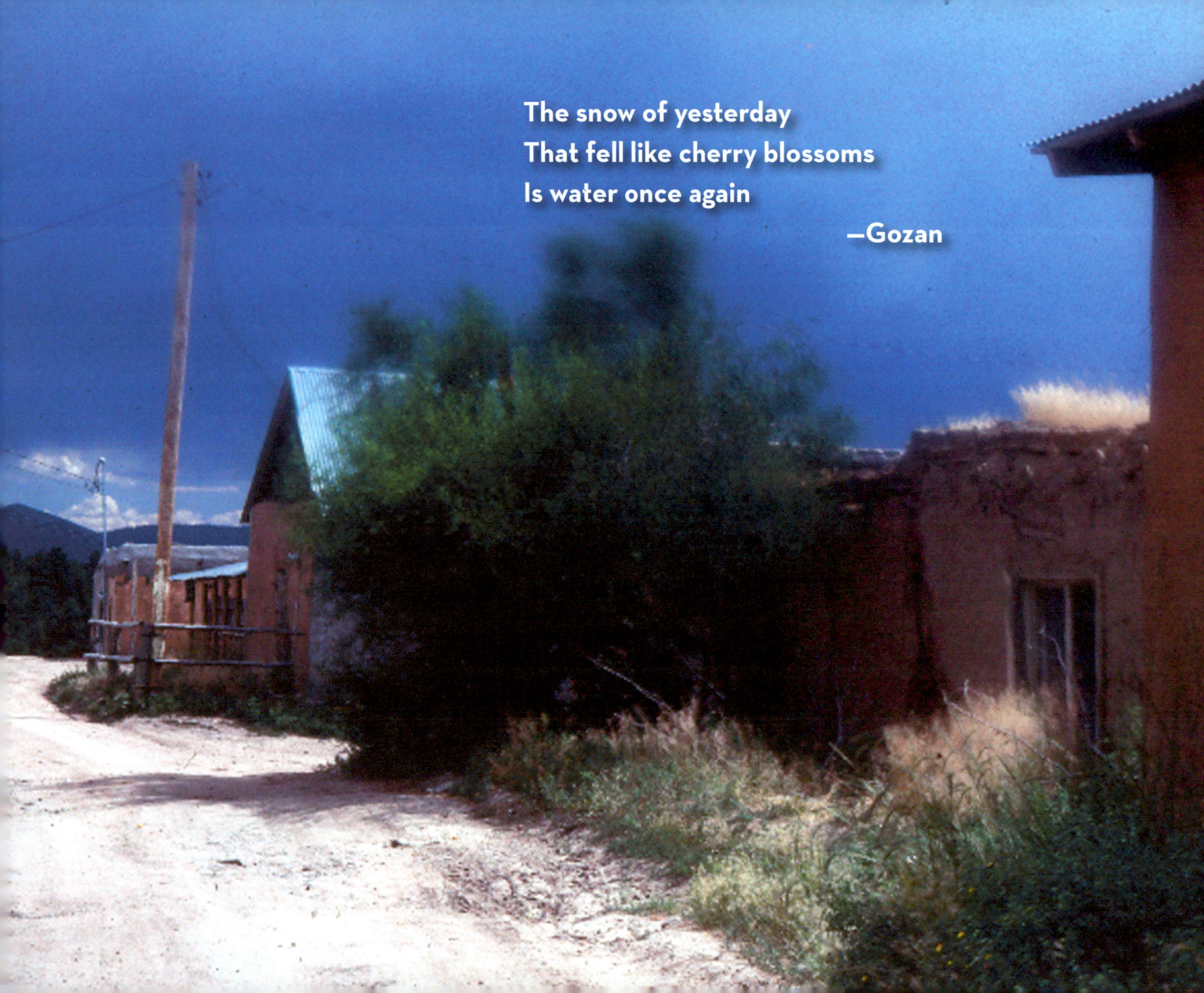

> The snow of yesterday
> That fell like cherry blossoms
> Is water once again
>
> —Gozan

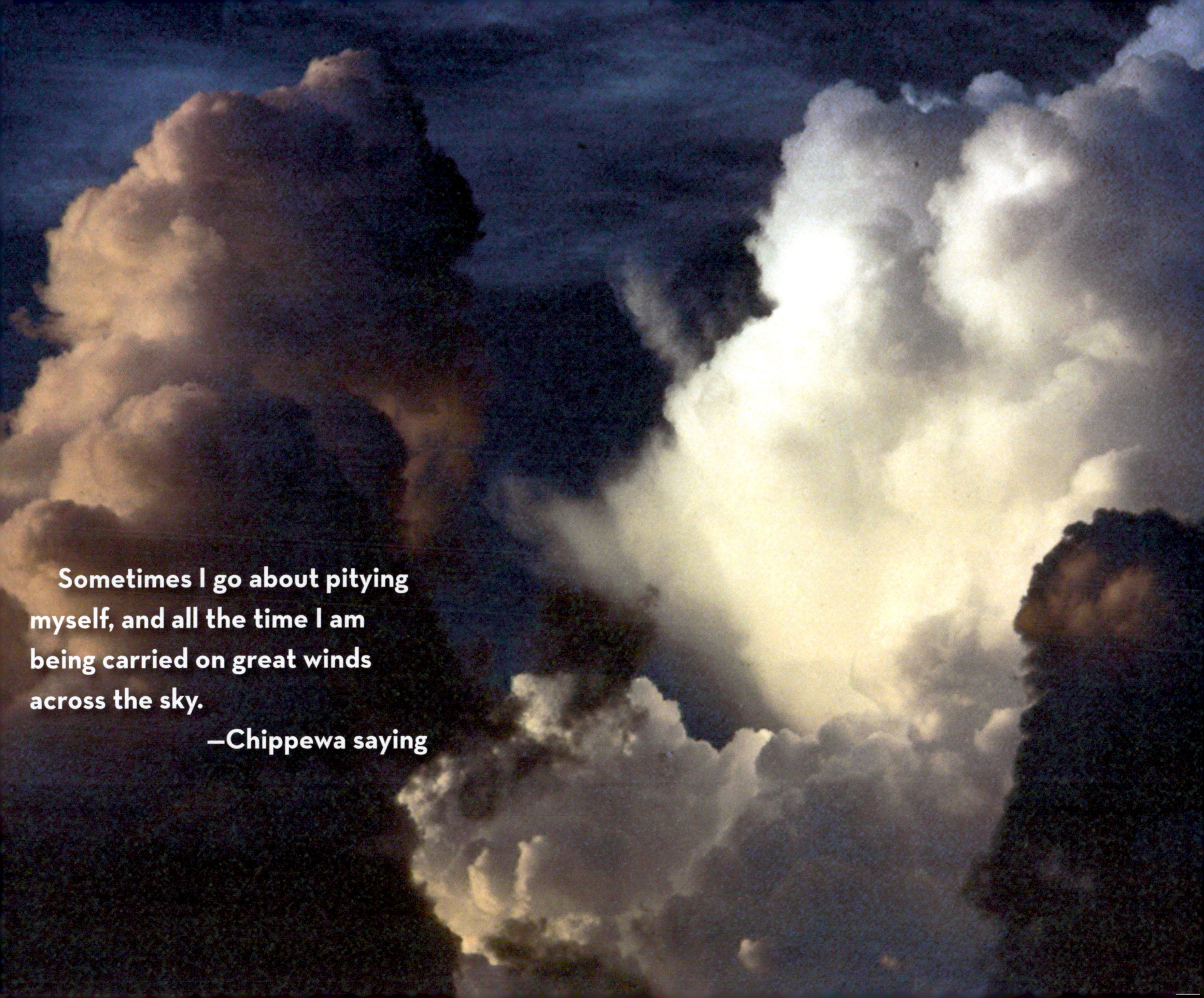

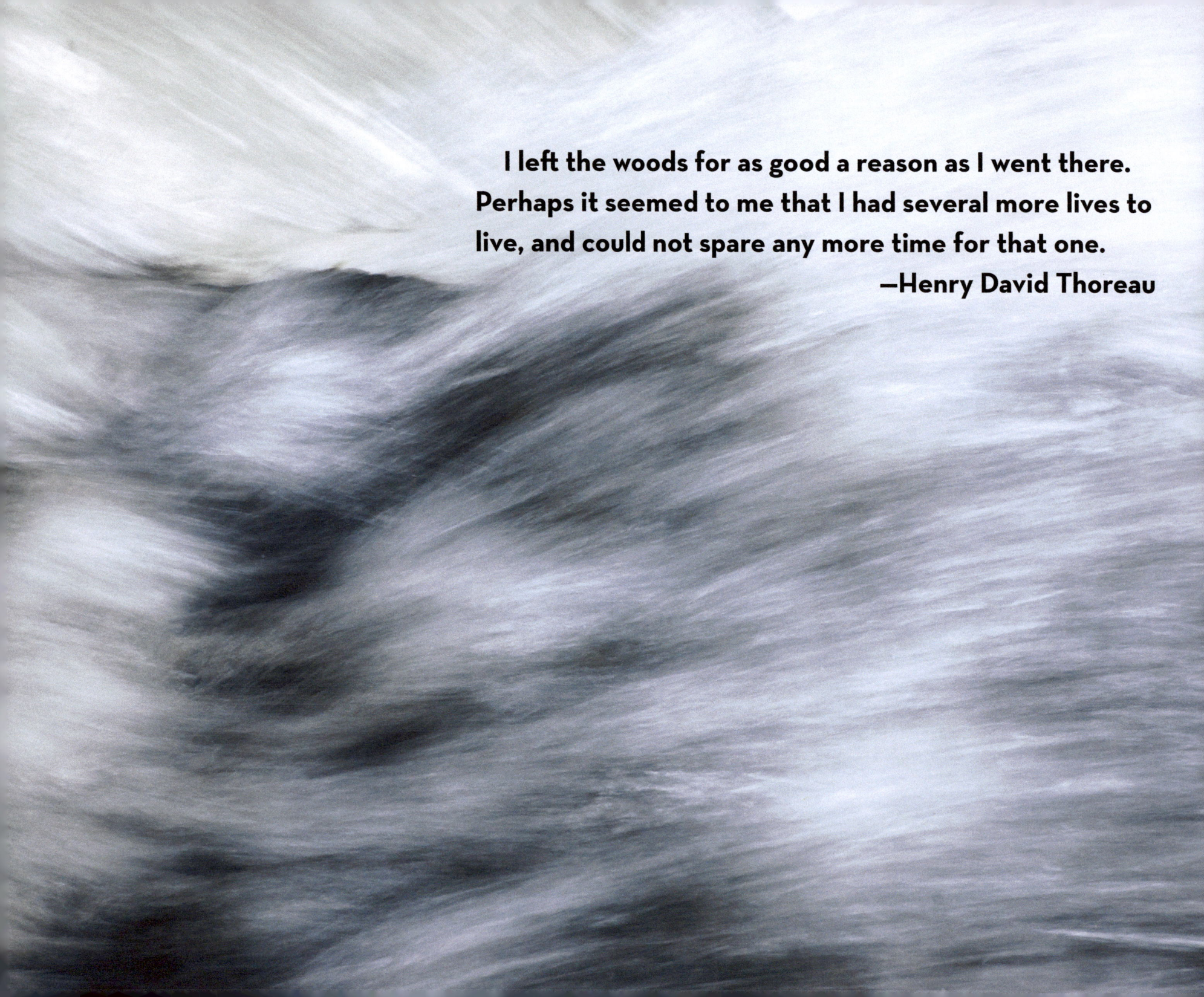

> I left the woods for as good a reason as I went there. Perhaps it seemed to me that I had several more lives to live, and could not spare any more time for that one.
> —Henry David Thoreau

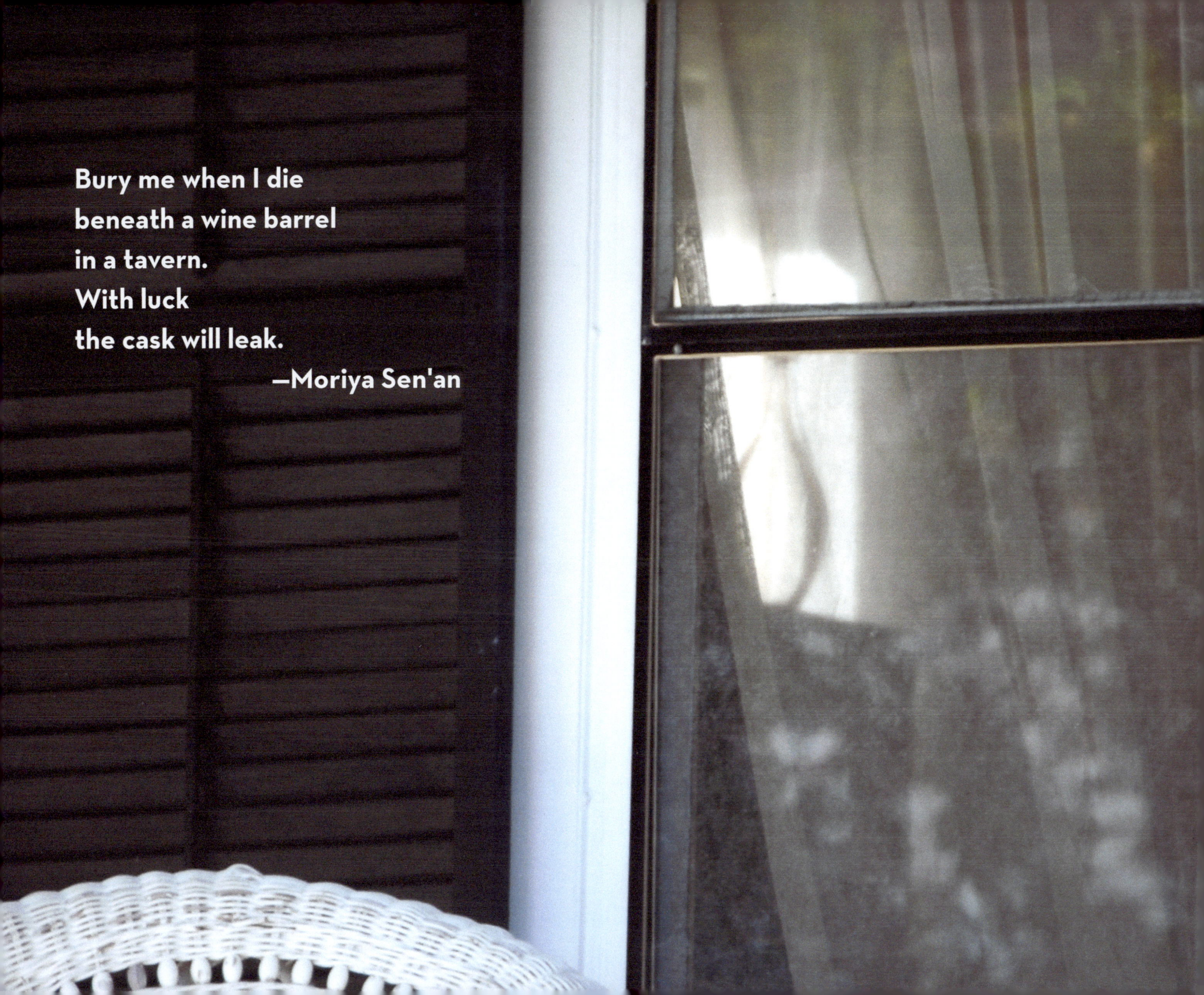

Bury me when I die
beneath a wine barrel
in a tavern.
With luck
the cask will leak.
—Moriya Sen'an

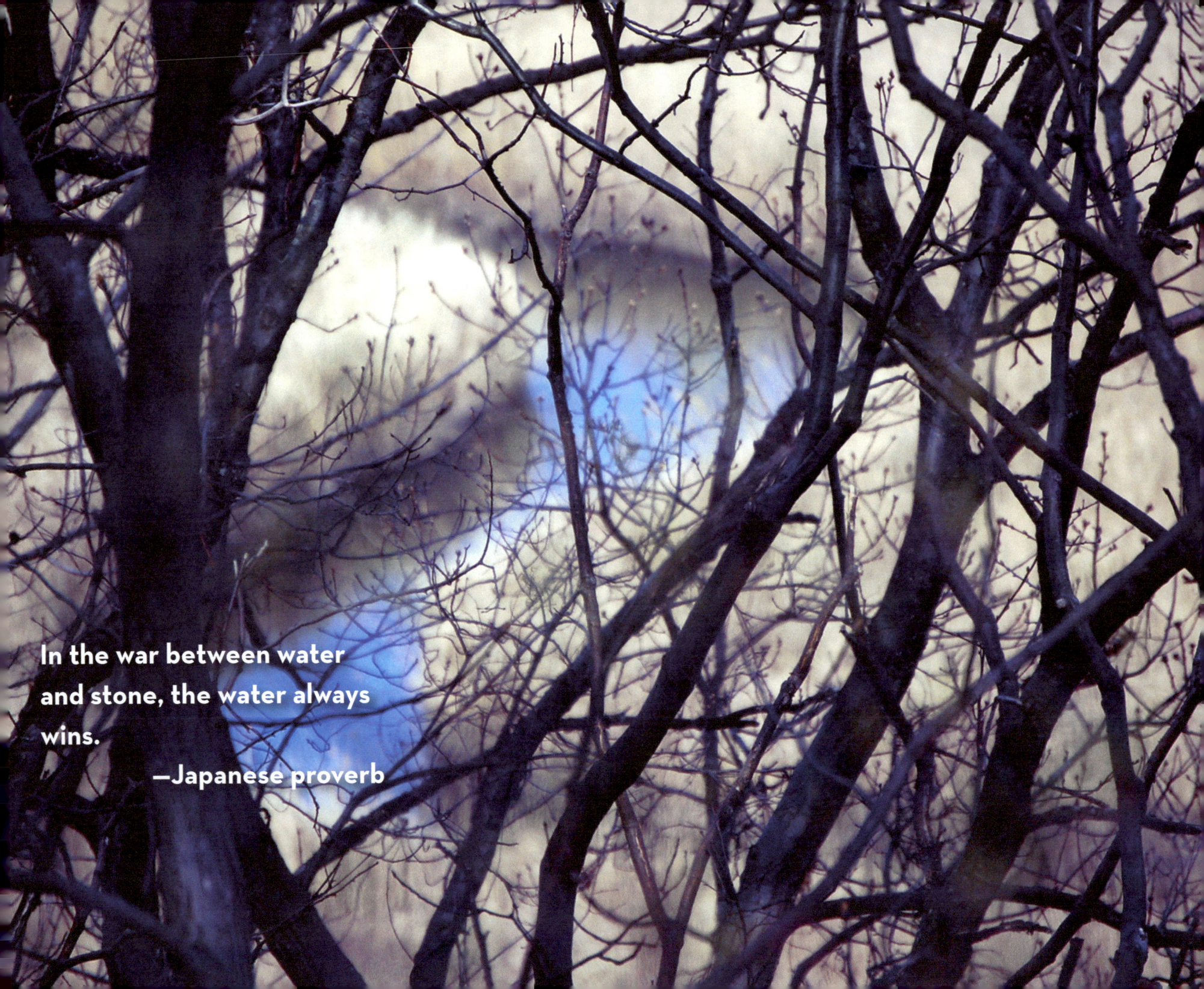

In the war between water and stone, the water always wins.

—Japanese proverb

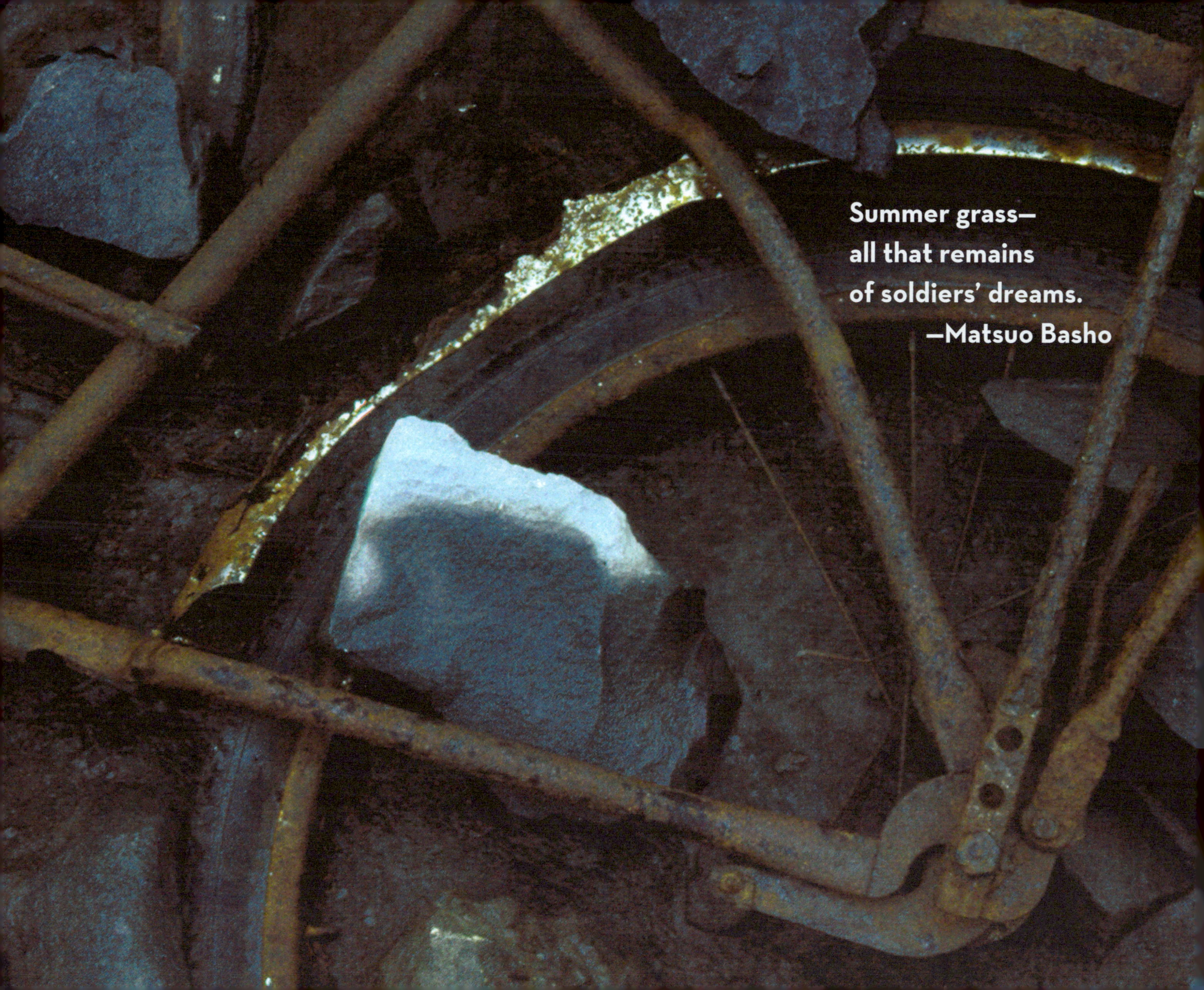

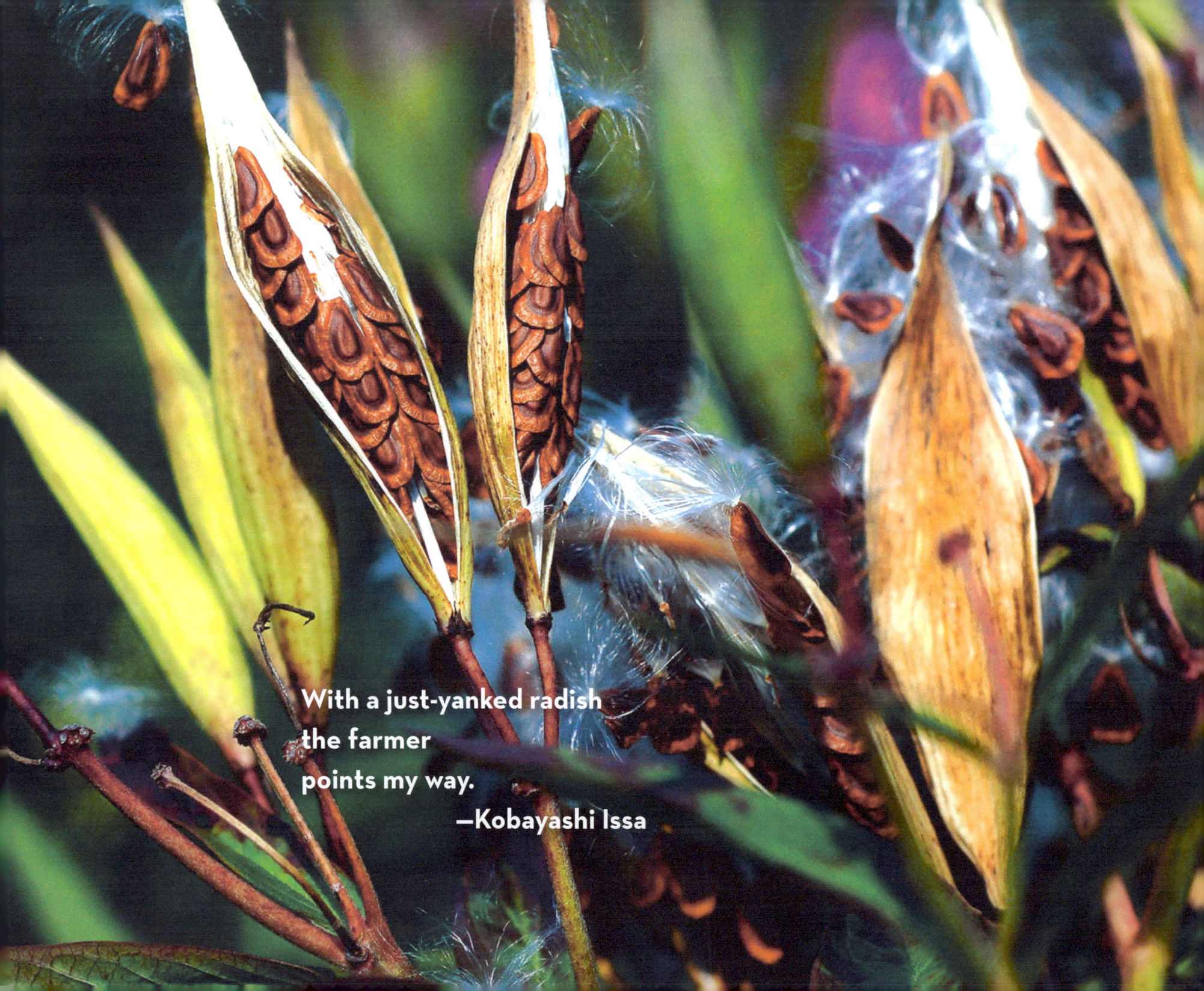

With a just-yanked radish
the farmer
points my way.
—Kobayashi Issa

ABOUT THE AUTHOR

This book is Barry Sheinkopf's eleventh in print. He has previously published mass-market fiction and nonfiction, poetry, a collection of photographs, and op-ed and other essays.

He is the director of The Writing Center in Englewood Cliffs, New Jersey, which he founded in 1977 and where he continues to teach professional writing courses.

He is also the publisher of Full Court Press (*fullcourtpress.com*), which currently has hundreds of titles on print, and has been an adjunct professor of English at the College of Staten Island for many years.

Mr. Sheinkopf has been an active member of The Authors Guild and Mystery Writers of America since 1989.

He lives in Northern New Jersey with his beloved wife, the writer and novelist Eugenia Koukounas.

www.ingramcontent.com/pod-product-compliance
Lightning Source LLC
Chambersburg PA
CBHW042320210526

45473CB00008B/2403